ELON MUSK

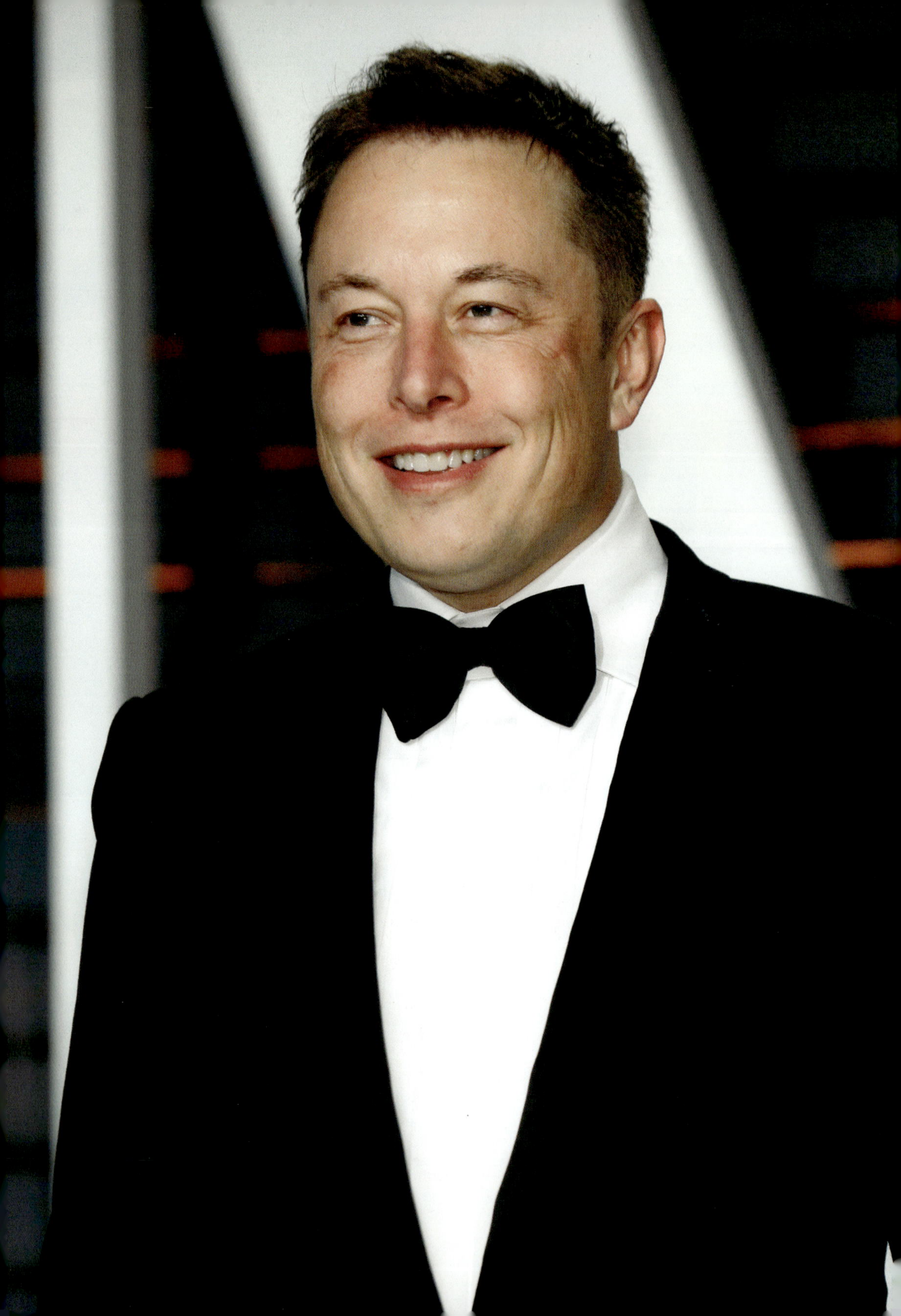

ELON MUSK

2ND EDITION

TITAN OF TECH AND BEYOND

PERCY LEED

Lerner Publications ◆ Minneapolis

Lerner Publications Company
An imprint of Lerner Publishing Group, Inc.
241 First Avenue North
Minneapolis, MN 55401 USA

For reading levels and more information, look up this title at www.lernerbooks.com.

Image credits: dpa picture alliance/Alamy, p. 2; AP Photo/Jordan Strauss/Invision, p. 6; AP Photo/Sciott Schilke/SIPA USA, p. 8; Finn stock/Shutterstock, p. 10; Tinxi/Shutterstock, p. 11; JHVEPhoto/Shutterstock, p. 12; Uladzik Kryhin/Shutterstock, p. 14; David Paul Morris/Bloomberg via Getty Images, p. 15; AP Photo/Paul Sakuma, p. 16; NASA, pp. 17, 23, 24; AP Photo/Jae C. Hong, p. 18; Image of sport/Alamy, p. 20; AP Photo/Mark Von Holden/SolarCity, p. 21; AP Photo/The Santa Maria Times, p. 22; AP Photo/Remy de la Mauviniere, p. 26; AP Photo/Reed Saxon, p. 27; AP Photo/Dave Bedrosian/Geisler-Fotopress/picture-alliance/dpa, p. 28; NASA/Bill Ingalls, p. 29; AP Photo/Robyn Beck/Pool Photo, p. 31; AP Photo/Refugio Ruiz, p. 34; AP Photo/Ringo H.W. Chiu, p. 35; AP Photo/STRMX, p. 37; AP Photo/Idrees Abbas/SOPA Images/Sipa USA, p. 38; Geopix/Alamy, p. 39; AP Photo/Evan Vucci, p. 40; Christopher Furlong/Getty Images, p. 41.
Cover: Chesnot/Getty Images.

Main body text set in Rotis Serif Std 55 Regular. Typeface provided by Adobe Systems.

Library of Congress Cataloging-in-Publication Data

The Cataloging-in-Publication Data for *Elon Musk, 2nd Edition: Titan of Tech and Beyond* is on file at the Library of Congress.
ISBN 979-8-7656-9054-3 (lib. bdg.)
ISBN 979-8-7656-9056-7 (pbk.)
ISBN 979-8-7656-9058-1 (epub)

Manufactured in the United States of America
1-1012014-54919-4/2/2025

TABLE OF CONTENTS

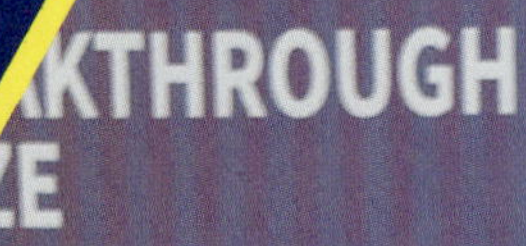

Musk smiles broadly in 2024, a year that saw him and his spacecraft company, SpaceX, often in the news.

On November 19, 2024, the tranquil air was suddenly filled with the roar of rocket engines coming to life. Smoke billowed out from underneath a 397-foot-tall (121 m) vehicle as it began to propel itself upward, launching into the sky from the Starbase located in Boca Chica, Texas. The vehicle was a massive rocket equipped with thirty-three Raptor engines that allowed it to climb out of the atmosphere for two and a half minutes before reversing course back toward the launch site. The heaviest rocket ever launched, it was fittingly called the Super Heavy Starship.

While the initial plan was for the Super Heavy to be caught by a giant set of arms, safety concerns led to a detour. It instead was directed to touch down in the Gulf of Mexico, where it appeared to be ready for a perfect landing before splashing into the water. The rocket was on its sixth successful test launch. This launch was to showcase both the rocket's maneuverability in critical moments as well as its ability to get out of Earth's lower atmosphere.

SpaceX's Super Heavy Starship IFT-6 launches on November 19, 2024.

Musk intently watched the rocket as it soared. His company SpaceX had created the Super Heavy. Other eyes were on the rocket too. The International Space Station (ISS) was passing overhead, and its crew could see the launch from space. Even President-elect Donald Trump joined Musk to see the rocket make its November test flight. Trump was interested in what SpaceX could do, and in the goal of getting to Mars. In a speech during his election campaign, he said, "Get those rocket ships going because we want to reach Mars before the end of my term. We want to do it." Musk liked Trump, and the feeling was mutual. And Musk was eager to take steps into the political world after all the work he'd done in technology.

Boy Wonder

Errol Musk, a mechanical and electrical engineer, and Maye Haldeman Musk, a fashion model and dietician, had three children. Their oldest child, Elon Reeve Musk, was born on June 28, 1971. Elon's brother, Kimbal, was born in 1972, and his sister, Tosca, was born in 1974. The Musk family lived in Pretoria in South Africa, a nation at the southern tip of the African continent.

Elon was a quiet and brainy boy. He loved reading, especially science fiction, fantasy, and stories about space travel. After school, he hung out at the local bookstore. His mom even called him "the encyclopedia" because he was always reading and absorbing information.

When Elon was eight years old, his parents separated. At first, he and his siblings lived with their mom in Durban, South Africa. But about two years later, Elon and Kimbal went to live with their dad in Johannesburg. Their dad taught them many engineering basics, such as how to run electrical wires into a house and how to install plumbing. "I'm naturally good at engineering . . . because I inherited it from my father," Musk said many years later. "What's very difficult for others is easy for me. For a while, I thought [mechanical and electrical] things were so obvious that everyone must know this." Elon's dad also taught him how to mix together chemicals to make explosives. Elon and Kimbal used that knowledge to build their own toy rockets made of canisters filled with gunpowder.

Musk lived with his dad in Johannesburg, South Africa. South Africa is Africa's southernmost country.

At the age of ten, Elon saw a personal computer (PC) for the first time. With his saved allowance, and with the help of his dad, he bought his first PC, a Commodore VIC-20. The machine came with instructions for programming in the BASIC computer language. Elon studied the book and mastered the instructions in three days. In 1984 twelve-year-old Elon used the PC to create code for a sci-fi computer game, which he called *Blastar*. A South African computer magazine paid him $500 for the code and published it for readers. The introduction in the magazine explained, "In this game you have to destroy an alien space freighter, which is carrying deadly Hydrogen Bombs and Status Beam Machines."

Musk's first computer was a Commodore VIC-20.

Elon's middle school years were hard for him. He was small, the youngest kid in his grade, and was bullied. He got through those tough years by putting his attention into learning more about computers. In high school, he continued to learn coding, mastering not only BASIC but also the COBOL and Pascal computer languages.

After graduating from high school, Musk enrolled at the University of Pretoria, where he studied engineering and physics. But by then he was hoping to leave South Africa. Silicon Valley, an area south of San Francisco, California, was the heart of the emerging personal computer industry. Musk hoped to work there someday, and he made a plan. His mother had grown up in Canada and was a Canadian citizen. That connection meant that Musk could become a Canadian citizen too. He decided to move to Canada as a first step and then move to its southern neighbor, the United States.

He moved to Canada in 1989. After working at a few odd jobs, he enrolled at Queen's University in Kingston, Ontario. His brother later followed, leaving South Africa and enrolling at the same university. In his spare time, Musk built computers from scratch and sold them to other students for less than they'd have to pay for

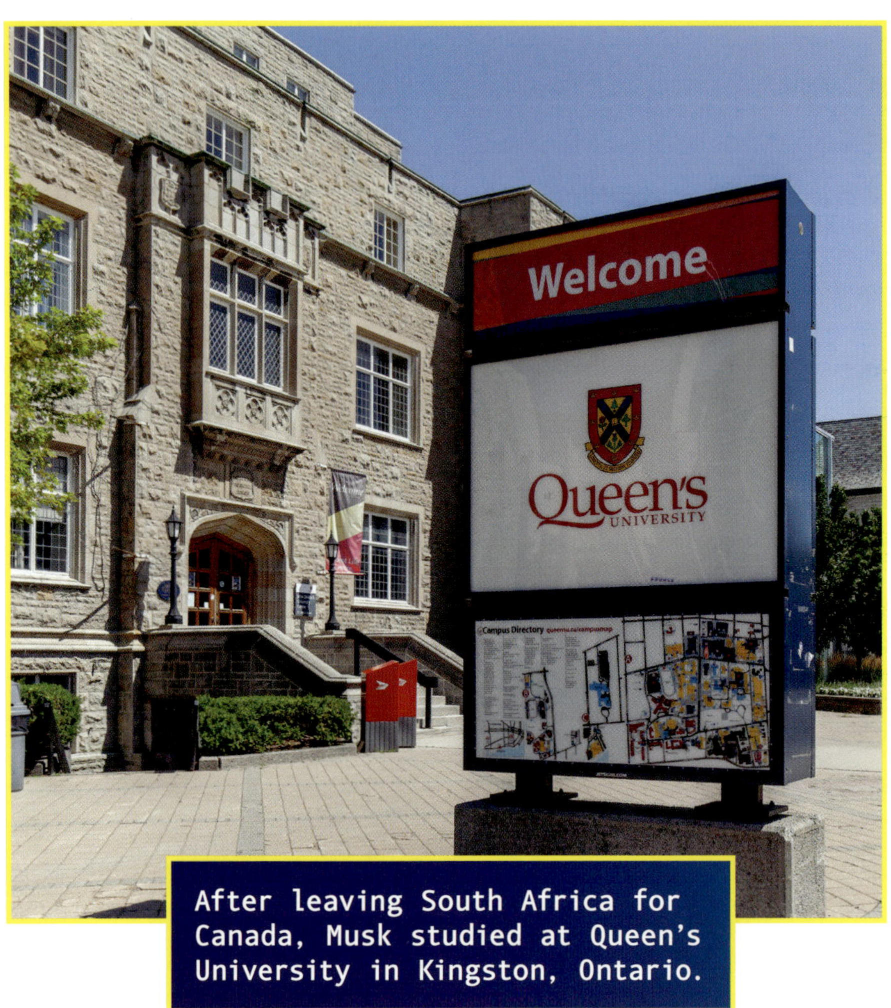

After leaving South Africa for Canada, Musk studied at Queen's University in Kingston, Ontario.

store-bought machines. He earned additional money by fixing computers. During his two years at Queen's University, Musk met fellow student Justine Wilson, who wanted to become a writer. The two began dating.

In 1992 Musk transferred to the University of Pennsylvania in Philadelphia. He chose the school for its top-notch reputation. Finally, he was able to move to the United States. Wilson remained in Canada, and the two had a long-distance relationship. At Penn, Musk continued to work hard and learn more about business and science. He impressed one professor with a paper on solar energy and solar power plants. He described a way to capture the sun's energy using solar collectors in space. He envisioned enormous devices, 2.5 miles (4 km) wide, sending solar energy to Earth via microwaves. In another paper, Elon wrote about ultracapacitors, devices that could store power for cars, airplanes, and rockets. He graduated from Penn with two bachelor's degrees, in physics and economics.

Fast Company

During the summer of 1994, Musk finally got to Silicon Valley. He interned with Pinnacle Research Institute in Los Gatos, California. He also interned at Rocket Science Games, which made video games with dazzling special effects. Musk's job there was to write computer code, but he often tackled extra work beyond his assigned tasks.

Many technology companies have their headquarters in Silicon Valley. Musk moved there in 1994.

Musk enrolled in a PhD program in engineering at Stanford University. This Silicon Valley–area school was a hub for the computer revolution in the 1990s, including brand-new internet communications. But after only a few days as a Stanford student, Musk realized that he didn't want to be in school studying technology. He wanted to be out in the business world, running his own technology company. He quit the PhD program.

His brother joined him in California, and in 1995 the two launched Global Link Information Network, later renamed Zip2. The company produced online city directories with business listings and maps to

Kimbal Musk (*pictured*) started Global Link Information Network in 1995 with his brother, Elon Musk.

help consumers find stores and services. The business prospered. When the computer company Compaq offered to buy Zip2 in 1999, the brothers sold it. Musk used part of his $22 million payout to start another business, X.com, an online banking company. He enjoyed his newfound wealth, buying a $1 million McLaren sports car and his own small airplane, which he learned to fly. In 2000 X.com merged with the online payment company Confinity, and the business was renamed PayPal. When eBay bought PayPal for $1.5 billion in 2002, once again Musk profited handsomely. This time, his payout was more than $150 million.

Musk (*right*) and PayPal cofounder Peter Thiel (*left*) pose with the PayPal logo in 2000.

By then Wilson had joined Musk in California. The two married in 2000. After the sale of PayPal, they left Silicon Valley for Los Angeles. He hoped to work in the aerospace industry, which had a strong base in LA.

In Los Angeles, Musk learned about an organization that wanted to build a human colony on Mars. He loved the idea. He devised a project, dubbed Mars Oasis, to send a private spacecraft to Mars. The spaceship would carry robotic greenhouses for growing plants on the Martian surface. As they grew, the plants would release oxygen,

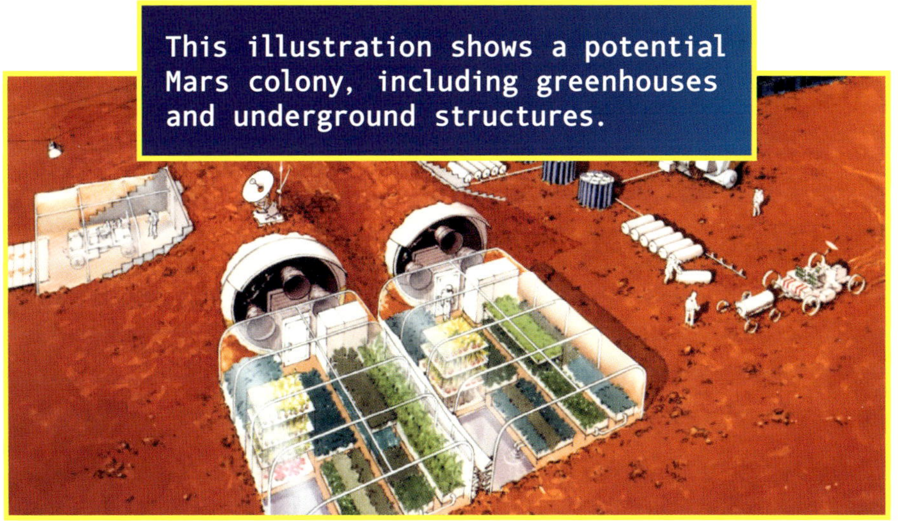

This illustration shows a potential Mars colony, including greenhouses and underground structures.

which would make the air on Mars breathable for future human colonists. Determined to carry out this plan, Musk and two colleagues traveled to Russia three times between 2001 and 2002 to try to buy the rocket they needed to launch a spacecraft. They met with Russian aerospace executives but came home each time without a deal. But Musk wasn't about to give up. He told his colleagues, "Hey, guys. I think we can build this rocket ourselves."

Musk teamed up with aerospace engineer Tom Mueller, who shared his interest in rocketry. At that time, only enormous companies built rockets. The biggest aerospace firms were Lockheed Martin and Boeing. They did business with the US National Aeronautics and Space Administration (NASA) and other government agencies. These firms employed tens of thousands of workers and secured multibillion-dollar government contracts. Their big, powerful rockets launched large satellites and space probes. Musk and Mueller saw a way to compete with

SpaceX, originally located in El Segundo, had its headquarters in Hawthorne, California, for many years.

these big firms. They envisioned a company that would build smaller, more efficient, and more affordable rockets to launch smaller payloads into space. In June 2002 they founded Space Exploration Technologies, or SpaceX, in El Segundo, California.

Electric Storm

While Musk worked hard to make SpaceX succeed, he kept tabs on other cutting-edge businesses. One of them was Tesla, a brand-new electric car company. Electric cars were not a new idea. Some of the first cars made in the 1800s ran on electricity. But gas-powered cars took over the market and dominated the automobile industry through most of the twentieth century. In the late 1990s, electric cars returned to the spotlight because they are more environmentally friendly than gas-powered cars.

Understanding Modern Climate Change

Earth's climate has changed over time but has seen a significant warming trend since the mid-twentieth century. Human activity, such as driving gas-powered cars and cutting down large forests, has increased levels of carbon dioxide (CO_2) and other greenhouse gases in the atmosphere. These gases trap the sun's heat, leading to rising temperatures on Earth.

Scientists say Earth's average surface temperature has risen more than 2°F (1°C) since 1880. Earth's higher temperatures are strengthening hurricanes and other storms and are causing more wildfires and droughts. Ocean temperatures are also increasing, causing polar ice to melt and sea levels to rise. According to NASA's Gravity Recovery and Climate Experiment (GRACE), Antarctica, which surrounds the South Pole, has lost an estimated 118 gigatons of ice every year since 2002. (One gigaton equals a billion metric tons.) And Greenland, which is near the North Pole, has lost an estimated 281 gigatons of ice everyyear.

Electric cars, which are powered by rechargeable batteries, use less energy than gas-powered cars, and they do not emit polluting gases and particles.

Tesla's cofounders, Martin Eberhard and Marc Tarpenning, wanted to take advantage of the growing interest in eco-friendly electric cars. But they weren't just interested in reducing pollution. They planned to build a high-performance, fast-as-lightning electric convertible. They called it the Roadster.

When Musk learned about the Roadster, he jumped on the Tesla bandwagon. He had long been interested in alternative energy sources, and he loved fast cars. In 2004 he invested millions of dollars in Tesla Motors and became board of directors chair and a company cofounder. Although others ran the day-to-day operations,

A 2002 Lotus Elise Mule 1. The Roadster's design was modeled after the Mule 1.

Musk oversaw Tesla's long-term planning and overall business strategy.

Musk's family grew tremendously during this time. Twin boys were born in 2004. Two years later, Musk's wife gave birth to triplets. While raising his suddenly big brood, Musk also helmed two cutting-edge technology businesses. He added a third in 2006 when he helped two of his cousins, Peter and Lyndon Rive, to start SolarCity, a solar energy company. Once again, Musk was a major investor and chaired the board of directors.

Musk and his cousins Peter Rive (*left*) and Lyndon Rive (*right*) deliver a speech in 2012. The three men started a solar energy business together in 2006.

Musk worked seven days a week, which didn't leave much time for his family. His marriage suffered, and the couple separated in 2008. They later divorced and agreed to share custody of their five children.

Blast Off!

SpaceX moved to One Rocket Road in Hawthorne, California. At the new site, aerospace mechanics worked in the center of the facility and engineers sat in offices nearby. The setup allowed the two groups to work closely together, bounce ideas off of one another, and exchange quick feedback. Rather than buying parts from suppliers, the team built almost all the components they needed,

Since starting SpaceX, Musk (*left*) keeps coming up with new ideas. Here, he talks to California Governor Gavin Newsom about plans for the Falcon Heavy.

including rocket engines and electronics. By bypassing outside suppliers, SpaceX saved money. They could make sure everything was up to their standards. Musk was driven to succeed. He often worked more than one hundred hours per week and pushed his staff to put in similarly grueling hours.

On September 8, 2008, the Falcon 1 launched and orbited Earth.

The company's early years were marked by frustration. Some of its first rockets failed on the launchpad. Others exploded in the air. It wasn't until September 2008 that SpaceX madc its first successful rocket launch. It put the Falcon 1 rocket into orbit around Earth, and the mission control team cheered. "My mind is kind of frazzled," exclaimed Musk after the rocket shot into the sky. "It's definitely one of the greatest days of my life, and probably for most people here. We've shown people we can do it. This is just the first step of many."

The Dragon spacecraft is attached by the Canadarm2 robotic arm at the ISS on May 25, 2012.

Further success came in December 2008, when the company won a $1.6 billion contract with NASA to make twelve supply flights to the ISS. For that, the SpaceX team designed a space capsule called Dragon. It would be able to carry not only cargo but also astronauts.

Over at Tesla, Musk and his engineers wanted to revolutionize the automobile business. Like SpaceX, they were building most parts from scratch. The team was working on the Roadster. It was designed to go from 0 to 60 miles (0 to 97 km) an hour in less than four seconds, on par with the fastest gasoline-powered sports cars. With a fully charged battery, it would be able to travel about 250 miles (402 km)—more than many other electric cars. Car lovers were excited about the Roadster. Long before it went into production, about nine hundred buyers, including actor George Clooney and then-California Governor Arnold Schwarzenegger, had preordered Roadsters. The price was a whopping $109,000.

Eco-Friendly Electric Cars

Most people drive gasoline-powered cars. Run by internal combustion engines, these vehicles release polluting gases and particles into the air. But some drive electric cars, which are more eco-friendly. Electric cars run on batteries, don't emit polluting gases, and use less energy to operate than gas-powered cars.

Cleaner fuel technology can make electric cars even more eco-friendly. Musk explained, "The great thing about electric cars is that you can generate the electricity from a wide range of renewable sources like hydro [water power], geothermal [heat from inside Earth], wind, [and] solar." To fight climate change, Musk would like to see electric cars—whether built by Tesla or another company—replace gasoline-powered cars completely. He says, "Until we see every car on the road being electric, we will not stop."

This Tesla Roadster was on display at an auto show in 2008.

But the road was rocky. The Tesla team struggled with production problems and delays. And in 2008, the United States entered a severe economic recession. Tesla nearly folded. But a $465 million loan from the US Department of Energy enabled Tesla to stay afloat and release the Roadster.

The Roadster was followed in June 2012 by the Model S, priced at a still-high $57,400. It was unlike any other car on the market. Inside, drivers found no knobs to turn or buttons to push. Instead, they controlled everything in the car via a laptoplike touch screen mounted next to the steering wheel. Instead of an internal combustion engine, power came from a

Musk presents the Tesla Model S in 2009.

giant slab of lithium ion batteries beneath the car floor. Drivers charged the batteries using home chargers. Away from home, they could use public charging stations that Tesla was building elsewhere. Some charging stations were solar powered. A fully charged Model S could travel 300 miles (483 km) between charges. In 2013 *Motor Trend* magazine named the Model S its Car of the Year—one of the highest honors in the automotive industry. The magazine *Consumer Reports* gave the car a high rating: 99 points on a scale of 100.

As his companies prospered, Musk became richer and more famous. He even made it to the big screen. He played himself in *Iron Man* 2 and in several TV shows.

Audiences enjoyed seeing Musk on-screen, but some coworkers found him hard to get along with. He demanded perfection from his staff. "Elon has a mind that's a bit like a calculator," said one Tesla manager. "If you put a number on the projector that does not make sense, he will spot it." He frequently fired staffers who made mistakes—even just grammatical errors in emails. At both Tesla and SpaceX, he battled with other top executives and board members. He fought for control and eventually became the chief executive officer (CEO) of both companies.

Musk attending the *Vanity Fair* Oscar party in 2015 in Beverly Hills, California

Musk had difficulties in his private life as well. He married British actress Talulah Riley in 2010, but the relationship had many ups and downs. The couple divorced, remarried, and divorced again, officially calling it quits in 2016.

Reaching for the Stars

Both Tesla and SpaceX prospered in the 2010s. Tesla introduced its most affordable car, the $35,000 Model 3. SpaceX built bigger and more powerful rockets. In May 2012 SpaceX sent the Dragon spacecraft to the ISS. It was the first private space vehicle ever to dock at the station. And in 2015 the team at SpaceX debuted perhaps the most jaw-dropping advance yet: a reusable rocket.

Up until then, space launch vehicles were used just once. Some rocket parts would fall back to Earth right away, while others would remain out in space, orbiting Earth for years until gravity eventually pulled them

Musk and then-NASA Administrator Charles Bolden speak next to the Dragon spacecraft after its return to Earth on May 31, 2012.

down. Then, the rocket remains usually grew fiery hot as they rubbed against gases in the air, caught on fire, and disintegrated.

Musk thought it was a huge waste. He explained, "The way rockets work right now is they are all expendable. So, you fly them once, and you throw it away." But with a reusable rocket, you reload fuel and fly again. Musk predicted that reusable rockets would lead to enormous cost savings: "If we could use the same Falcon 9 rocket a thousand times, then the capital costs would go from being $60 million per flight to $60,000 per flight. Obviously, that's a humongous difference."

The SpaceX engineers designed a rocket that would release its payload into space, loop around, and then fall back toward Earth in a vertical alignment. Engines would fire to slow the rocket as it gently touched down on four 25-foot (7.6 m) landing legs. After that, the rocket could be refilled with fuel and used again. After a number of failures, SpaceX successfully landed a first-stage Falcon 9 booster rocket, first on land and then on a platform at sea, in late 2015 and early 2016. The company first reused a previously flown rocket in March 2017.

By this time, SpaceX was launching a rocket about once a month, carrying supplies for the ISS and satellites for telecommunications companies and government agencies. Tesla was also cruising at high speed. It built a giant facility in Nevada, called the Gigafactory, to produce lithium ion batteries for its cars.

Idea Man

Los Angeles is infamous for its crowded freeways and traffic jams. A trip that takes only fifteen minutes in light traffic can take more than an hour during rush hour. That traffic bothered Musk. So he thought of a solution. In December 2016 he founded a business called the Boring Company. Musk and other company leaders hope to build underground tunnels to enable high-speed transportation within Los Angeles and between LA and other cities. The vehicles that move through the tunnels will be similar

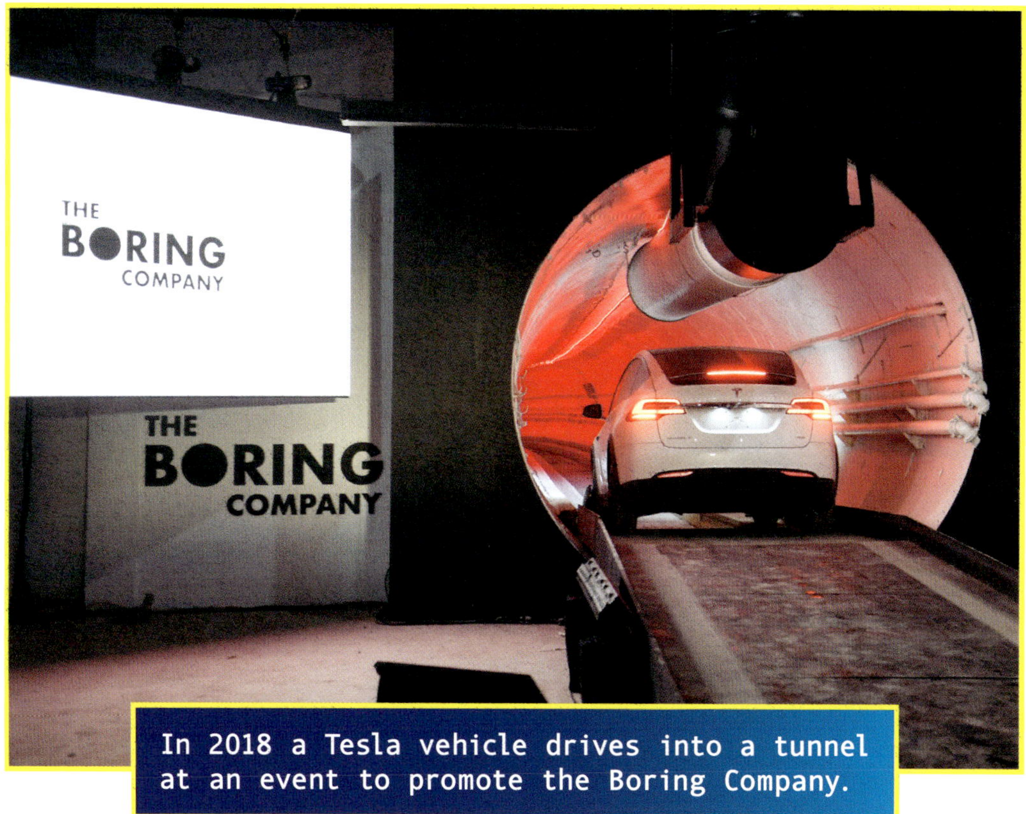

In 2018 a Tesla vehicle drives into a tunnel at an event to promote the Boring Company.

to subway cars, but they will go much faster: about 150 miles (241 km) per hour compared with an average of 20 miles (32 km) per hour for a subway car.

For even faster transportation, Musk proposed a system called Hyperloop. It would consist of passenger pods shooting through vacuum tubes at more than 700 miles (1,127 km) per hour. Initially, engineers from Tesla and SpaceX worked on Hyperloop, but Musk wanted to involve others. He made Hyperloop an open-source project, so outside businesses can develop and build on the technology. Some companies, including the Boring Company, are still working to make the Hyperloop a reality someday. Others believe it is impractical and will never come to fruition.

Musk made one of his most daring proposals on September 27, 2016, at the meeting of the International Astronautical Congress in Mexico. In a speech titled "Making Humans a Multiplanetary Species," he announced his goal of establishing a human colony on Mars. He said that humans should become a multiplanet species, especially since climate change and other catastrophes threatened to make Earth uninhabitable. "If we were a multiplanetary species, that would reduce the possibility of some single event, man-made or natural, taking out civilization as we know it, as it did the dinosaurs," he later explained to a reporter. "It's insurance of life as we know it, and it makes the future far more inspiring if we are out there among the stars and you could move to another planet if you wanted to."

How to Make a Mars Colony

Musk is excited about sending humans to Mars. He said, "It's the grandest adventure I could possibly imagine. . . . I couldn't think of anything more exciting, more fun, more inspiring for the future than to have a base on Mars." But can it really be done? After all, Mars has little water, no breathable air, deadly radiation from the sun, and temperatures as low as −200°F (−129°C). So starting a colony there will be challenging. Here are just a few of the steps that we could take:

- **Extract water from the icy Martian soil for drinking and growing plants.**
- **Turn some of the water into oxygen for breathable air.**
- **Build underground dwellings and greenhouses to protect colonists and plants from radiation.**
- **Release underground gases into the Martian atmosphere to trap heat from the sun and to raise the planet's temperature.**

Many scientists say that even if all this could be done, it would take up to a thousand years to make Mars suitable for living things.

Musk, at the International Astronautical Congress on September 27, 2016, talks about colonizing Mars.

Musk spoke out against artificial intelligence, saying that machines that are more intelligent than humans could endanger civilization. But Musk was not against all AI. Tesla was pushing ahead on self-driving cars, which rely on artificial intelligence to make decisions in the place of human drivers. And in 2016 Musk cofounded Neuralink, which hopes to implant AI-based computer chips into human brains. This technology might help to restore eyesight, hearing, movement, or other functions to those with injuries or impairments.

Driving Forward

Cars weren't the only vehicle type Musk wanted to showcase through Tesla. He wanted to show the range of what electric cars could be. Even as far back as 2012, he wanted Tesla to create the best electric pickup truck.

Finally, they were able to show their prototype in November of 2019. The Cybertruck looked like something out of a video game, with straight lines and a shiny, silver exterior. Musk wanted something like Bladerunner. Some people criticized this look, disliking how different it was from traditional vehicles. At the demonstration, Tesla claimed the windows were virtually unbreakable. However, two shattered when Franz von Holzhausen, a vehicle designer at Tesla, threw metal balls at them.

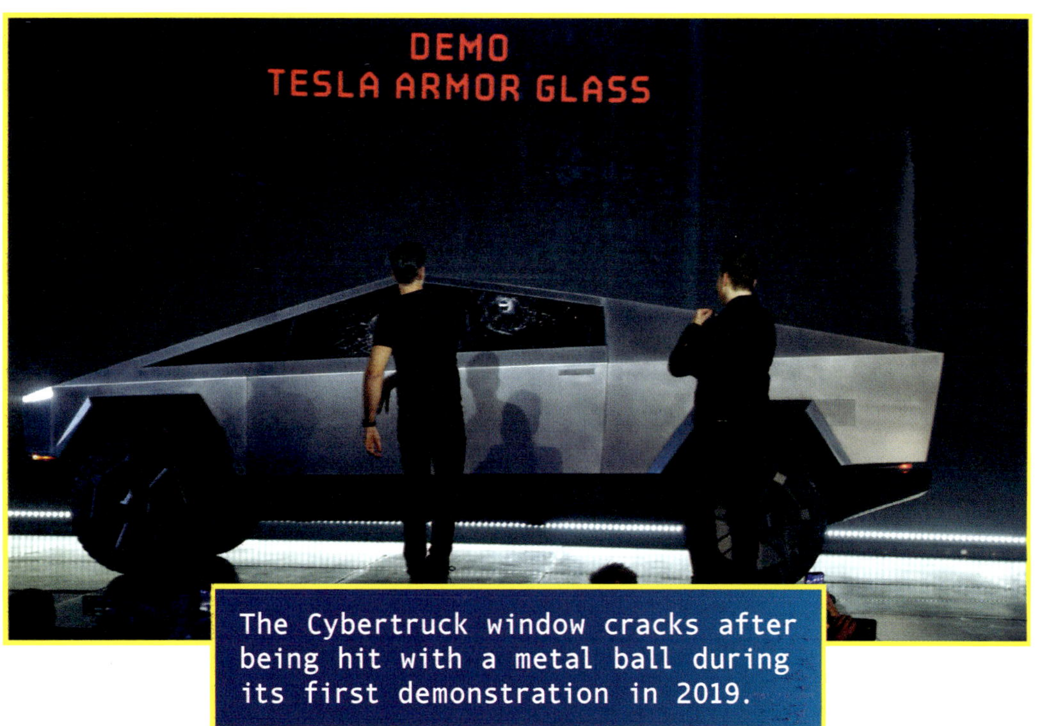

The Cybertruck window cracks after being hit with a metal ball during its first demonstration in 2019.

Tesla's Namesake

Tesla founders Martin Eberhard and Marc Tarpenning named their company in honor of Nikola Tesla, a Serbian American pioneer in the electrical power industry. Tesla was born in Austria-Hungary (modern-day Croatia) in 1856. After studying engineering for several years, Tesla developed a power generator that used alternating current (AC). This is an electric current that reverses direction many times each second. In the United States, inventor Thomas Edison was the first person to build electric power plants and to run electrical lines to homes and businesses. Edison's equipment ran on direct current (DC), which flows in only one direction. In 1884 Tesla moved to the United States. He tried to convince Edison and others that AC was better than DC for electrical power distribution. Tesla's AC system proved superior to DC and came into widespread use.

A newspaper story published in 1934 says that Tesla invented an electric car that ran without batteries. The story has been widely repeated, but historians say it isn't true. Tesla never built a car, but he did invent several other devices, including electric motors. He also experimented with X-rays, radar, lighting, and remote control.

Despite the critiques, there were still many people who made reservations to get a Cybertruck. Musk claimed that at least 250,000 reservations had been made by the end of the first month. He said the trucks would be available by 2021, but production was difficult. People began to receive their Cybertrucks in 2023. But it seemed the Cybertruck was plagued with issues. Within the first year of its release, it had seven separate recalls. One issue was with the accelerator pedal, which could dislodge and become trapped. People worried that the shape of the truck and the stainless-steel exterior could cause more injuries or damage if a Cybertruck were to hit a pedestrian or other vehicle on the road.

Musk attending the 2018 Costume Institute Benefit Gala at the Metropolitan Museum of Art

Social Media Man

In 2022 Musk set his sights on social media. Rather than create his own social media website, he wanted to use an existing platform.

The platform he wanted to use was then known as Twitter.

He liked the website a lot, so much that he wanted to have a say in how it ran. He considered himself an avid believer in absolute freedom of speech. He didn't like the ban Twitter had on Donald Trump at the time. He wanted to get rid of the many bot accounts—accounts which aren't run by a real person and can contribute to spam and misinformation. "I think Twitter is currently the best, or looked at another way, the least bad public square, a forum for the exchange of ideas, nationally and internationally. But I think it could be a lot better at that," he stated.

Musk's profile and the X logo

He offered to buy the website for $44 billion. Some celebrated, believing that conservative opinions were being censored on the platform. They thought Musk would stop that from happening. Others were concerned. They believed that the website's current rules were essential to stopping hate speech.

Musk became Twitter's CEO in October 2022. One thing he wanted to do was change the name. He decided that Twitter would be known as X.

As the 2020s went on, Musk became a more polarizing figure. The issues with the Cybertruck and his purchase of Twitter created a divide in opinions. Some loved him

British politician and member of Parliament Rishi Sunak interviews Musk about artificial intelligence in November 2023.

Musk attends Donald Trump's presidential campaign rally on Saturday, October 5, 2024, prior to the 2024 presidential election.

for everything he had accomplished in technology and his politics. Others were unsure about his political views and how he handled his desire for absolute freedom of speech.

Musk also became a vocal supporter of Republicans and conservative movements. In 2022 he decided he would no longer support Democrats. As the 2024 US presidential election drew closer, he endorsed then-candidate Donald Trump.

In August of 2024, Musk and Trump spoke on an X livestream. Musk suggested an efficiency commission for the government. Trump liked the idea. After being elected, he offered Musk a position to lead the Department of Government Efficiency. Musk was excited. He wanted to make sure productivity and efficiency in the government were the best they could be. In 2025 Musk's department began slashing federal services and firing government employees. Thousands lost their jobs. Around the US, protestors spoke out against the changes.

While the department was set to expire in July of 2026, Musk was looking to cut $2 trillion in spending by that time. Whether or not he can reach that goal remains to be seen. But Musk has a long track record of achieving his goals and making his dreams come true.

Musk speaks during the 2025 presidential inauguration.

IMPORTANT DATES

1971	Elon Musk is born in Pretoria, South Africa.
1984	Elon writes code for a sci-fi computer game called Blastar.
1989	Musk moves to Canada and enrolls in Queen's University in Ontario.
1992	Musk transfers to the University of Pennsylvania.
1995	Musk and Kimbal Musk launch Zip2, an online business directory.
1999	Musk founds the online banking company X.com, which later becomes PayPal.
2002	Musk founds SpaceX.
2004	Musk invests in Tesla Motors and chairs its board of directors.
2008	SpaceX successfully launches a rocket into orbit for the first time.

2012	Tesla introduces the Model S. SpaceX sends a Dragon spacecraft to the ISS.
2015	SpaceX lands a reusable rocket for the first time.
2016	Musk founds the Boring Company to build tunnels for underground transportation. He announces plans to build a human colony on Mars.
2018	SpaceX first launches its Falcon Heavy rocket, which carries a cherry-red Roadster and a dummy named Starman.
2019	Tesla demonstrates the first Cybertruck prototype.
2020	SpaceX sends astronauts to the International Space Station.
2022	Musk purchases the website Twitter and renames it X.
2023	The first Cybertrucks hit the road.
2025	Musk leads the Department of Government Efficiency under President Donald Trump.

SOURCE NOTES

8 William Harwood. "SpaceX launches Super Heavy-Starship on 6th test flight, with Trump in attendance. Here's what to know." *CBS News*, November 19, 2024, https://www.cbsnews.com/news/spacex-starship-launch-6-what-to-know/.

9 Sissi Cao, "At 71, Elon Musk's Model Mom, Maye Musk, Is at Her Peak as a Style Icon," *Observer*, January 7, 2020, https://observer.com/2020/01/elon-musk-mother-maye-model-dietician-interview-book-women-self-help/.

9 Neil Strauss, "Elon Musk: The Architect of Tomorrow," *Rolling Stone*, November 15, 2017, https://www.rollingstone.com/culture/culture-features/elon-musk-the-architect-of-tomorrow-120850/.

10 Ashlee Vance, *Elon Musk: Tesla, SpaceX, and the Quest for a Fantastic Future* (Ecco, 2015), 30, e-book.

17 Vance, 119.

23 Christian Davenport, *The Space Barons: Elon Musk, Jeff Bezos, and the Quest to Colonize the Cosmos* (PublicAffairs, 2018), 144.

25 “Elon Musk: I’ll Put a Man on Mars in 10 Years,” YouTube video, 16:34, posted by *Wall Street Journal*, December 27, 2011, https://www.youtube.com/watch?v=IiPJsI8pl8Q&feature=emb_title.

25 “‘Until we see every car on the road being electric, we will not stop’—Elon Musk,” YouTube video, 0:23, posted by Mark Sita, March 4, 2019, https://www.youtube.com/watch?v=bqf26thSK7Q.

28 Vance, 220.

30 Davenport, 198.

30 Stephen L. Petranek, *How We’ll Live on Mars* (Simon and Schuster, 2015), 33, e-book.

32 Strauss.

33 “Elon Musk ‘Mars Pioneer Award’ Acceptance Speech—15th Annual International Mars Society Convention,” YouTube video, 33:00, posted by the Mars Society, August 9, 2012, https://www.youtube.com/watch?v=PK0kTcJFnVk&feature=emb_title.

38 Peter Campbell. “Future of the Car: Elon Musk Interview,” *Financial Times* video, 0:23, May 10, 2022, https://www.ft.com/video/1bf5c3d6-fdf1-4a24-975e-c58aa5bb0d1a.

SELECTED BIBLIOGRAPHY

Belfiore, Michael. "Behind the Scenes with the World's Most Ambitious Rocket Makers." *Popular Mechanics*, September 1, 2009. https://www.popularmechanics.com/space/rockets/a5073/4328638/.

Davenport, Christian. *The Space Barons: Elon Musk, Jeff Bezos, and the Quest to Colonize the Cosmos*. PublicAffairs, 2018.

Gunter, Joel. "Elon Musk: The Man Who Sent His Sports Car into Space." BBC News, February 9, 2018. https://www.bbc.com/news/science-environment-42992143.

Hayes, Adam. "Who Is Elon Musk?" Investopedia. Last modified March 5, 2025. https://www.investopedia.com/articles/personal-finance/061015/how-elon-musk-became-elon-musk.asp.

Niedermeyer, Edward. *Ludicrous: The Unvarnished Story of Tesla Motors*. BenBella Books, 2019.

Petranek, Stephen L. *How We'll Live on Mars*. Simon and Schuster, 2015. e-book.

Strauss, Neil. "Elon Musk: The Architect of Tomorrow," *Rolling Stone*, November 15, 2017. https://www.rollingstone.com/culture/culture-features/elon-musk-the-architect-of-tomorrow-120850/.

Vance, Ashlee. *Elon Musk: Tesla, SpaceX, and the Quest for a Fantastic Future*. Ecco, 2015, e-book.

LEARN MORE

Alternative Energy
https://c03.apogee.net/mvc/home/hes/land/el?utilityname=gru&spc=kids&id=16183

Hirsch, Rebecca E. *Mysteries of Mars.* Lerner Publications, 2021.

Leed, Percy. *Donald Trump, 2nd Edition: Unprecedented Politician.* Lerner Publications, 2025.

NASA for Students in Grades 5–8
https://www.nasa.gov/learning-resources/for-students-grades-5-8/

Roach, Mary. *Packing for Mars for Kids.* Norton Young Readers, 2022.

Safe Return
https www.timeforkids.com/g56/safe-return/

INDEX